BL5.9

Science & Technology
HALL OF FAME

Morgan Hughes

The Rourke Book Company, Inc.
Vero Beach, Florida 32964

© 2001 The Rourke Book Company, Inc.
All rights reserved. No part of this book may be reproduced or utilized in any form or by any means, electronic or mechanical including photocopying, recording, or by any information storage and retrieval system without permission in writing from the publisher.

PHOTO CREDITS
Cover, pages 4-7, 10-19, 22 © Archive Photos, New York, NY; page 9: Courtesy of the International Space Hall of Fame, Almagordo, NM; page 21: Courtesy of the National Teachers Hall of Fame, Emporia, KS

EDITORIAL SERVICES:
Janice L. Smith for Penworthy Learning Systems
Pamela Schroeder

PRODUCED & DESIGNED BY:
East Coast Studios
ecs@megabits.net

Library of Congress Cataloging-in-Publication Data

Hughes, Morgan, 1957–
    Science and technology / Morgan E. Hughes.
        p. cm. — (Halls of fame)
    Includes index.
    Summary: Describes six Halls of Fame that honor special people and accomplishments in science and technology, including the National Inventors Hall of Fame, the International Space Hall of Fame, and the Ecology Hall of Fame.
    ISBN 1-55916-270-8
    1. Science museums—United States—Juvenile literature. 2. Industrial Museums—United States—Juvenile literature. 3. Halls of Fame—United States—Juvenile literature. [1. Science museums. 2. Industrial museums. 3. Halls of Fame. 4. Museums.] I. Title
Q105.U5 H84 2000
507.4'73—dc21
                                                                                    00–023890

Printed in the USA

Table of Contents

National Inventors Hall of Fame..............5

International Space Hall of Fame 8

Ecology Hall of Fame 11

Army Aviation Hall of Fame...................14

National Aviation Hall of Fame 17

National Teachers Hall of Fame 20

Glossary 23

Index..24

National Inventors Hall of Fame

The National Inventors Hall of Fame (NIHF) honors creative men and women who use their imaginations. These people have turned their imaginations into important or useful inventions we use every day.

The NIHF began in 1973. The NIHF honors **inventors** (in VENT urz) for their work. It also helps people learn about these clever men and women.

Alexander Graham Bell, born in Scotland, is one of the most important inventors in all of American history.

The first man in the NIHF was Thomas Alva Edison. He has been joined by such famous inventors as Alexander Graham Bell, George Washington Carver, George Westinghouse, Jr., and Orville and Wilbur Wright.

Orville and Wilbur Wright first flew in their invention, the Kitty Hawk.

President Bill Clinton said "yes" to building the Inventure Place.

The National Inventors Hall of Fame is located at 221 S. Broadway Street, Akron, OH 44308. Find out more about the NIHF at the website *http//invent.org*.

International Space Hall of Fame

The International Space Hall of Fame (ISHF) is part of The Space Center in Almagordo, New Mexico. The ISHF opened in 1976 to care for and show important objects in the history of space **exploration** (EK splawr RAY shun). New members join the Hall of Fame each October. There are five floors in the museum. Each one has its own displays.

You may contact The Space Center by writing to P.O. Box 533, Almagordo, NM 88311, by calling 800-545-4201, or by visiting its website at *www.zianet.com/space.*

The International Space Hall of Fame has five floors of displays that celebrate space exploration.

Ecology Hall of Fame

Did you know the word "**ecology**" (ee KAWL oh jee) was first used by German scientist Ernst Haeckel?

Now the Ecology Hall of Fame (EHF) is still in **cyberspace** (SIE ber SPAYS). However, there are plans to build a museum in Santa Cruz County, California. The new building will be a national center for **environment** (in VIE ruhn ment) education. The museum will have displays to teach people how to take care of the world.

The Ecology Hall of Fame is being built by EcoTopia/USA. This company in California wants everyone to think and act with the environment in mind.

Known as a great leader, Theodore Roosevelt was also a champion for ecology.

11

The Hall of Fame honors men and women who are heros who work to save the environment. Such people include the famous underwater filmmaker Jacques Cousteau and writer Henry David Thoreau.

Jacques Cousteau's underwater film-making opened up the world beneath the waves to millions of people.

Henry David Thoreau was a world famous poet who wrote about people and nature.

You can learn more about the Ecology Hall of Fame and read an interesting story about the history of ecology by visiting the EHF website at *www.ecotopia.org/ehof/about.html.*

Army Aviation Hall of Fame

One of the first men in the Army **Aviation** (AY vee AY shun) Hall of Fame was Russian helicopter maker Igor Sikorsky. He helped create a new way to fly, using the rotary wing.

The Army Aviation Hall of Fame is located at Fort Rucker, Alabama, in the Army Aviation Museum. The Hall displays pictures of early members, including winners of the Congressional Medal of Honor.

Learn more by visiting the website *www.quad-a.org/#top* and clicking on Hall of Fame, or by calling the Army Aviation Association National Office at 203-226-8184.

Igor Sikorsky changed how we fly forever with his rotary wing helicopters.

National Aviation Hall of Fame

In 1964, President Lyndon B. Johnson gave the National Aviation Hall of Fame (NAHF) its **charter** (CHAHRT ur). Since then, more than 150 heroes of aviation have joined. Among the many honored are pilots, astronauts, teachers, scientists, engineers, and inventors.

The NAHF covers aviation in the 20th century. It starts with the Wright Brothers (the first men to fly) and goes through John Glenn (the first man to orbit the Earth in space). War hero and test pilot Chuck Yeager and moon walker Neil Armstrong are also honored.

Amelia Earhart, Anne Lindbergh, Claire Chennault, and Ruth Rowland Nichols are among the great people included in the NAHF.

The "re-usable" shuttle was created after years of research by scientists in space exploration.

You can visit the National Aviation Hall of Fame website at *www.nationalaviation.org* and see pictures of all the members. You can read about what each member did.

Amelia Earheart's plane disappeared during a 1937 flight over the Pacific Ocean and was never found.

The Wright Brothers—Orville and Wilbur—were aviation leaders who flew the first airplane.

For more information, write to the National Aviation Hall of Fame at P.O. Box 31096, Dayton, OH 45437 or call 937-256-0944.

National Teachers Hall of Fame

Is there a teacher who means a great deal to you? Almost everyone has a favorite teacher.

The National Teachers Hall of Fame honors the men and women who serve the nation's children from preschool to 12th grade, in both public and private schools. These men and women have given their all to the important job of teaching.

You can visit this cyberspace Hall of Fame at *www.nthf.org.*

For more information contact the National Teachers Hall of Fame at 1320 C of E Drive, Emporia, KS 66801 or call 800-968-3224.

They may look like regular people, but these members of the Teachers Hall of Fame are super teachers.

GLOSSARY

aviation (AY vee AY shun) — the making or flying of aircraft

charter (CHAHRT ur) — written document that creates and defines an organization, like a Hall of Fame

cyberspace (SIE ber SPAYS) — a modern way of saying "on the internet"

ecology (ee KAWL oh jee) — the study of how people, plants, and animals live in their environment

environment (in VIE ruhn ment) — the place in which something lives

exploration (EK splawr RAY shun) — the careful and complete study of a place or idea

inventor (in VENT ur) — someone who makes something new

On March 10, 1876, Alexander Graham Bell said the famous words, "Mr. Watson, come here. I want you." He was using the first telephone.

INDEX

Armstrong, Neil   17
Army Aviation
   Hall of Fame   14
Bell, Alexander
   Graham   6
Carver, George
   Washington   6
Chennault, Claire   17
Congressional
   Medal of Honor   14
Cousteau, Jacques   12
Earhart, Amelia   17
Ecology Hall
   of Fame   11
Edison, Thomas Alva   6
Glenn, John   17
Haeckel, Ernst   11
International Space
   Hall of Fame   8

Johnson, Lyndon B.   17
Lindbergh, Anne   17
National Aviation
   Hall of Fame   17
National Inventors
   Hall of Fame   5
National Teachers
   Hall of Fame   20
Nichols, Ruth R.   17
Sikorsky, Igor I.   14
Thoreau, Henry
   David   12
Westinghouse,
   George Jr.   6
Wright, Orvill   6, 17
Wright, Wilber   6, 17
Yeager, Chuck   17